DYSCALCULIA MATH WORKBOOK

Angeline Gormley

D1532217

Welcome to Dyscalculia Math Workbook. Dyscalculia is a condition where an individual has difficulties grasping the symbols and operations involving math. With the use of this dyscalculia toolkit and worksheets, you will help break down the process of teaching the foundations of math.

This dyscalculia toolkit for kids contains detailed instructions, prompts, activities, and worksheets that will help you teach math creatively and to lessen the frustration between you and your child. When looking for dyscalculia books, dyscalculia math materials, this workbook is one of the earliest ones you can use to prepare children for more advanced lessons in the future.

This dyscalculia workbook can be reproduced as worksheets once purchased, and we donate to St. Jude's Hospital and Tim Tebow Foundation for children.

NUMBERS AND NUMBER WORDS

These animals need the other parts of their bodies. Pair the numbers with the right number words.

These animals need the other parts of their bodies. Pair the numbers with the right number words.

Please match the numbers with the right number words.

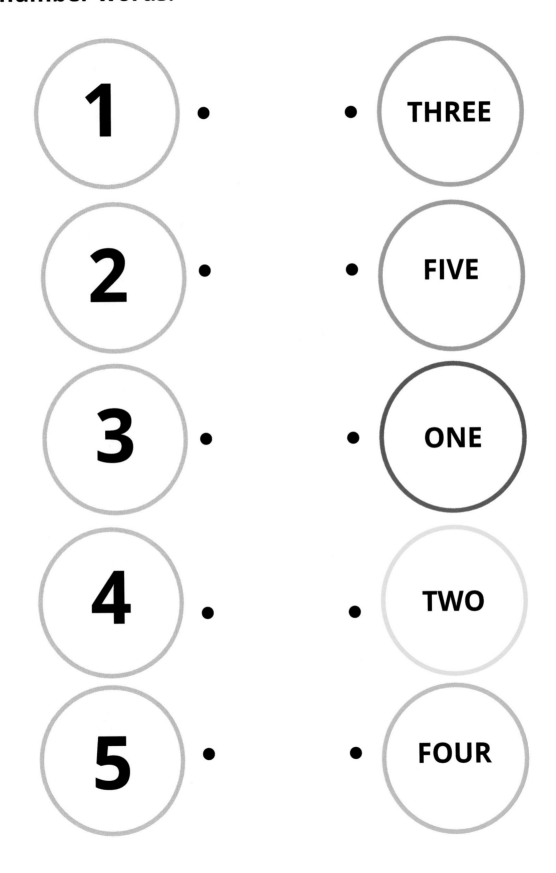

Please match the numbers with the right number words.

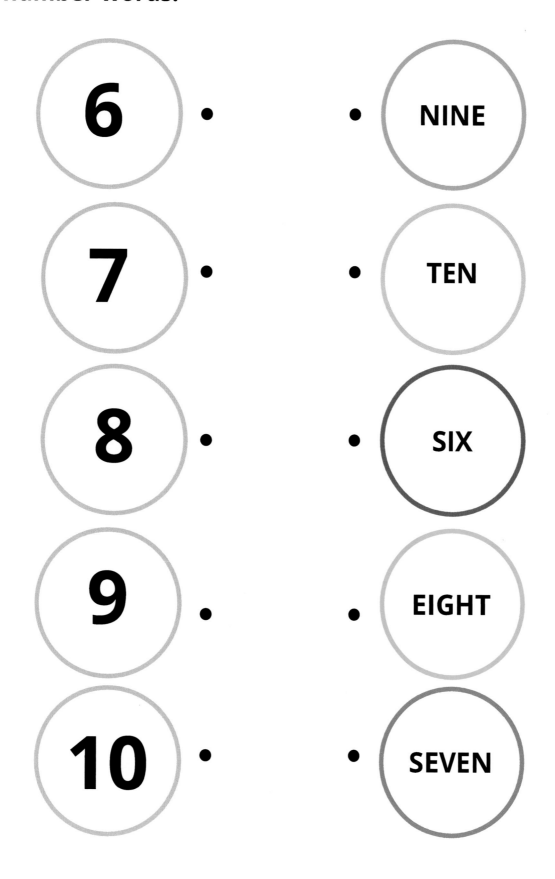

COUNTING

How many things are in each row? Let's count them one by one, starting from left to right. Color the correct answer.

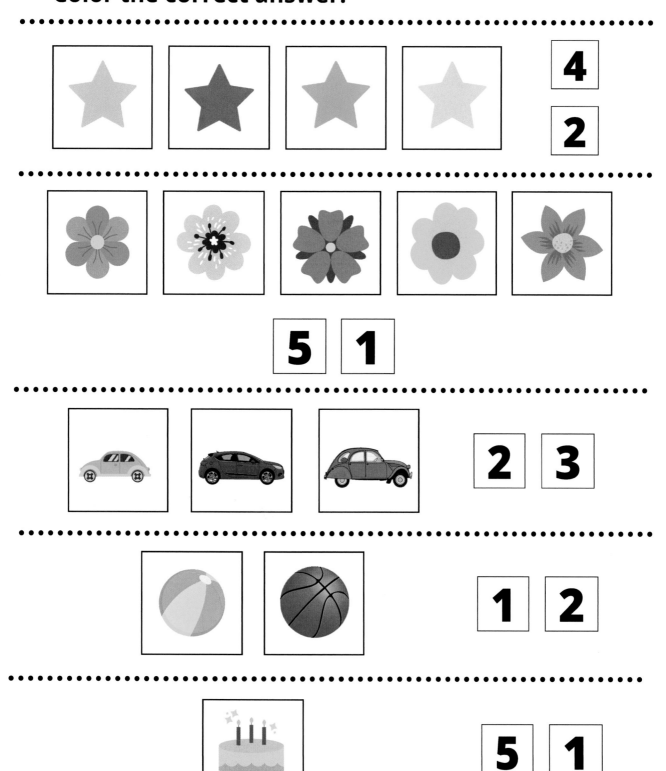

How many things are in each column? Let's count them one by one, starting from top to bottom. Color the correct answer.

10 **6**

9 **7**

8 **10**

7 **9**

8 **6**

How many things are there? Color the correct answer.

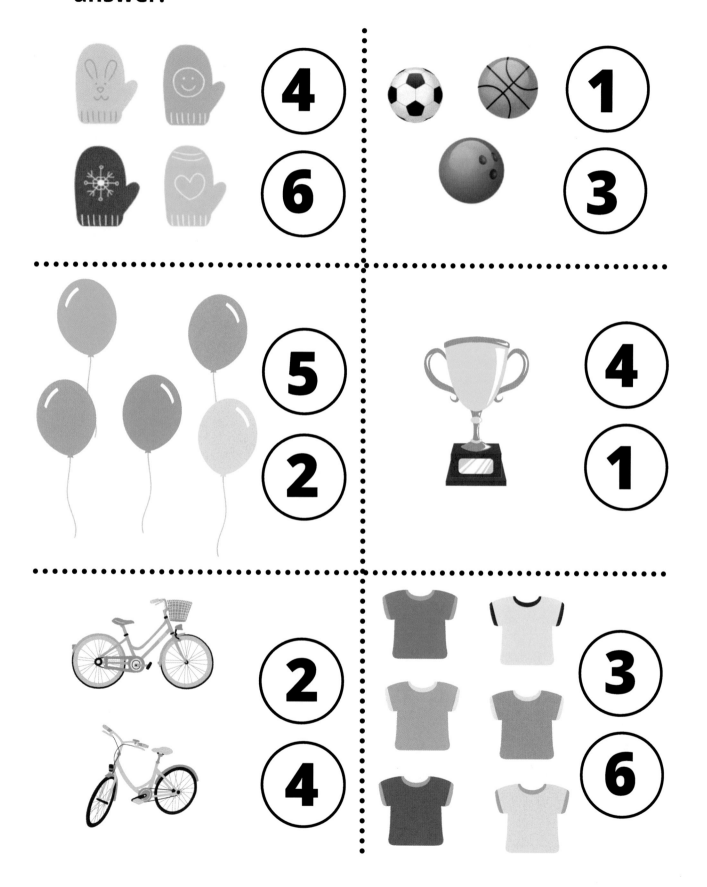

How many things are there? Color the correct answer.

How many things are there? Color the correct answer.

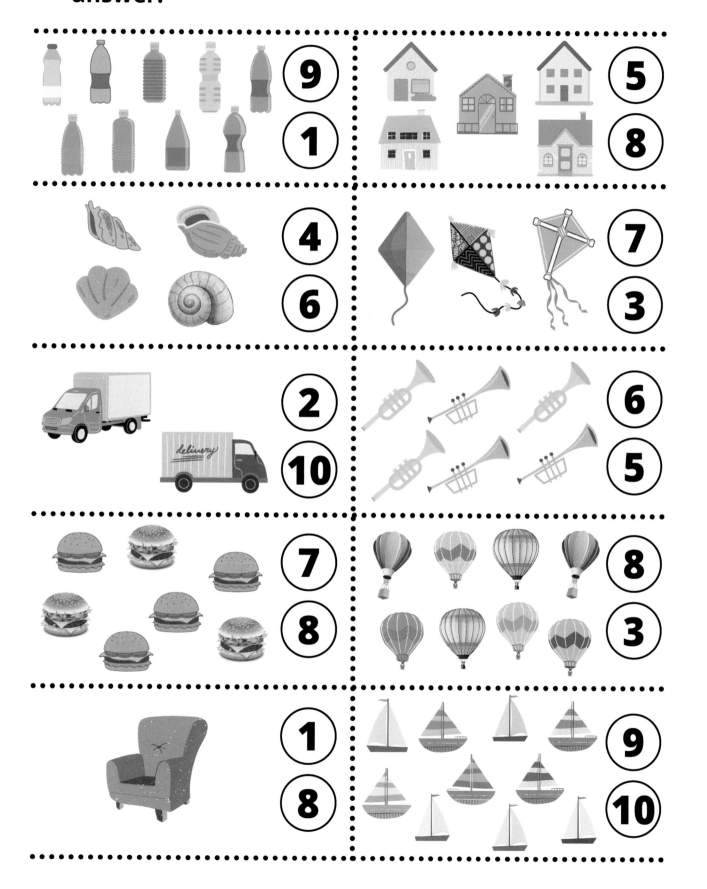

ADDITION

Addition is combining things to know how many there are. We combine the addends, count them together, to get the sum.

The parts of an
ADDITION NUMBER SENTENCE

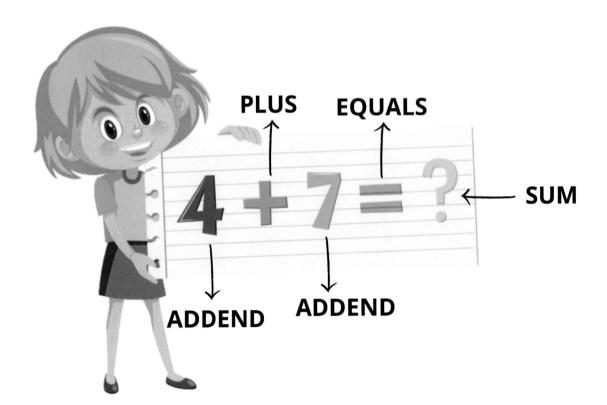

PLUS   EQUALS

4 + 7 = ?   SUM

ADDEND   ADDEND

Addition Equations

Find the sum by adding the items together.

2 + 2 = ___

4 + 1 = ___

1 + 2 = ___

3 + 1 = ___

1 + 1 = ___

2 + 3 = ___

Addition Equations

Find the sum by adding the items together.

2 + 1 = ___

0 + 5 = ___

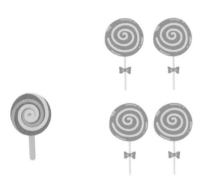

1 + 4 = ___

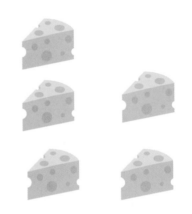

3 + 2 = ___

1 + 3 = ___

4 + 0 = ___

Addition Equations

Find the sum by adding the items together.

5 + 1 = ___

3 + 5 = ___

6 + 3 = ___

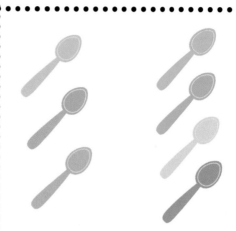

3 + 4 = ___

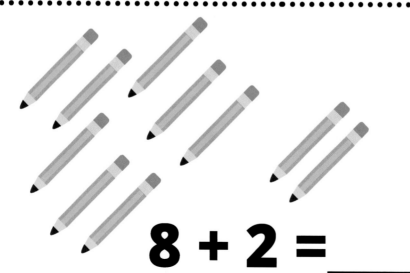

8 + 2 = ___

Addition Equations

Find the sum by adding the items together.

5 + 4 = ___

4 + 2 = ___

7 + 1 = ___

5 + 2 = ___

6 + 4 = ___

Addition Word Problems

Read the word problem and create the equation below. Also, draw the picture of items to count the addends together and find out the sum.

Sally and Liza picked apples from their garden. Sally got 4 red apples while Liza got 3 green apples. How many apples do they have altogether?

Picture:

Equation:

_____ + _____ = _____

In a fish tank there are 7 small fish and 2 large fish. How many fish are in the tank?

Picture:

Equation:

_____ + _____ = _____

At the zoo I saw 1 elephant standing and 2 elephants walking in their cage. How many elephants did I see?

Picture:

Equation:

_____ + _____ = _____

Addition Word Problems

Read the word problem and create the equation below. Also, draw the picture of items to count the addends together and find out the sum.

Dan has 5 cookies. He bought 4 more. How many does he have now?

Picture:

Equation:

_____ **+** _____ **=** _____

Elsa saw 6 butterflies in the garden. She saw 2 more flying near her. How many butterflies did she see?

Picture:

Equation:

_____ **+** _____ **=** _____

The chicken laid 8 eggs. Another chicken laid 2 eggs. How many eggs are there?

Picture:

Equation:

_____ **+** _____ **=** _____

SUBTRACTION

Subtracting means taking away an amount from a given number of items. These are the parts of a subtraction equation:

SUBTRACTION NUMBER SENTENCE

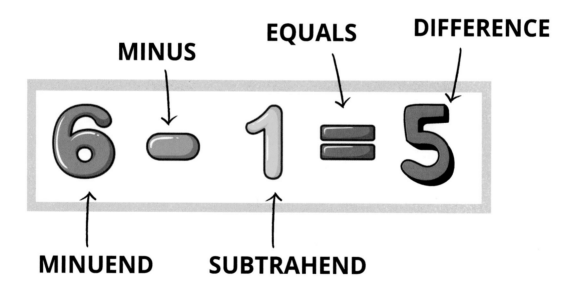

To answer a subtraction equation, you must take away from subtrahend from the minuend.

Subtraction Equations

Look at the pictures and subtraction equations below. Take away from subtrahend from the minuend, count what is left, and put the answer beside the equal sign.

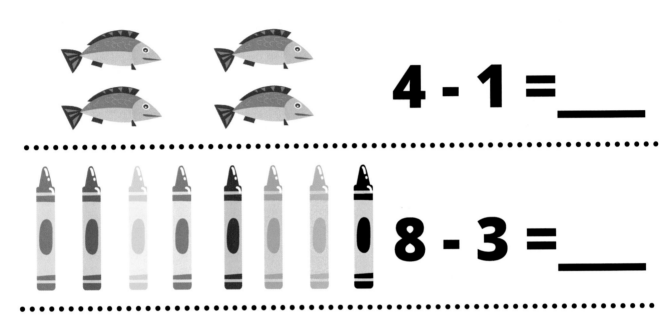

$4 - 1 =$ ___

$8 - 3 =$ ___

$3 - 3 =$ ___

$2 - 1 =$ ___

$5 - 2 =$ ___

Subtraction Equations

Look at the pictures and subtraction equations below. Take away from subtrahend from the minuend, count what is left, and put the answer beside the equal sign.

$$4 - 3 = \underline{\quad}$$

$$6 - 3 = \underline{\quad}$$

$$7 - 2 = \underline{\quad}$$

$$4 - 2 = \underline{\quad}$$

$$5 - 1 = \underline{\quad}$$

Subtraction Equations

Look at the pictures and subtraction equations below. Take away from subtrahend from the minuend, count what is left, and put the answer beside the equal sign.

8 - 2 = ___

6 - 4 = ___

9 - 1 = ___

10 - 3 = ___

7 - 1 = ___

Subtraction Equations

Look at the pictures and subtraction equations below. Take away from subtrahend from the minuend, count what is left, and put the answer beside the equal sign.

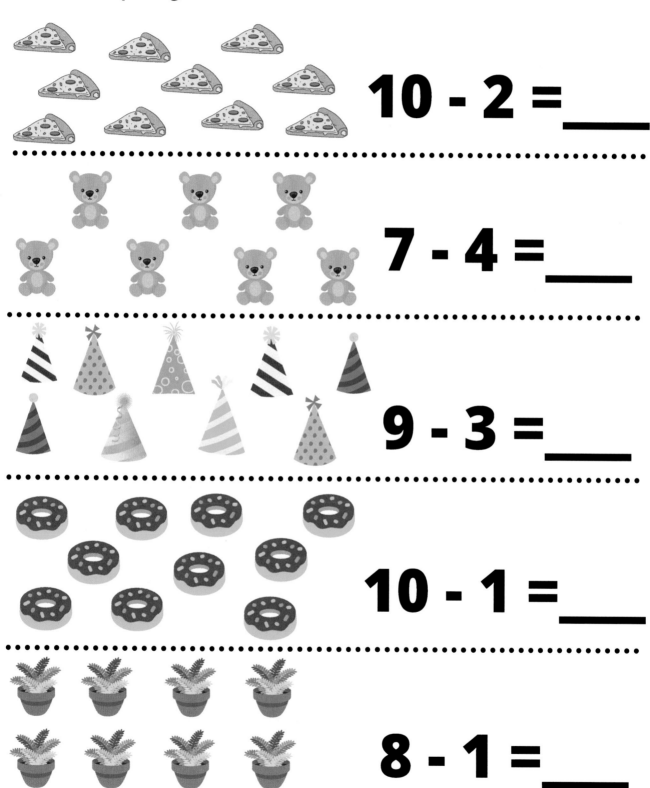

10 - 2 = ___

7 - 4 = ___

9 - 3 = ___

10 - 1 = ___

8 - 1 = ___

Subtraction Word Problems

Read each subtraction word problem, and draw the number of minuends. After that, cross out the subtrahend and count what is left. Also, write the equation below along with the difference.

There are 10 birds in a cage. Tim opened the cage and 6 flew away. How many birds were left?

Picture:

Equation:

_____ - _____ = _____

My mother baked 8 chocolate cup cakes. I ate 3 of them. How many cup cakes were left?

Picture:

Equation:

_____ - _____ = _____

Mary had 5 fresh flowers. She gave 2 to her sister. How many flowers were left?

Picture:

Equation:

_____ - _____ = _____

Subtraction Word Problems

Read each subtraction word problem, and draw the number of minuends. After that, cross out the subtrahend and count what is left. Also, write the equation below along with the difference.

Mrs. Smith had 5 umbrellas. She gave away 4 to her friends. How many does she have now?

Picture:

Equation:

_____ - _____ = _____

Bill had 7 marbles. He lost 3 of them. How many does he have now?

Picture:

Equation:

_____ - _____ = _____

I saw 9 starfish on the beach. I threw 7 of them back to the sea. How many were left on the sand?

Picture:

Equation:

_____ - _____ = _____

Subtraction Word Problems

Read each subtraction word problem, and draw the number of minuends. After that, cross out the subtrahend and count what is left. Also, write the equation below along with the difference.

Mr. Brown had 9 books. He gave 3 to his students. How many books does he have left?

Picture:

Equation:

_____ - _____ = _____

There are 10 pencils in my bag. I gave 2 to my friend. How many are left?

Picture:

Equation:

_____ - _____ = _____

I saw 8 balloons in the sky. The wind blew 1 away and was gone. How many were left?

Picture:

Equation:

_____ - _____ = _____

Subtraction Word Problems

Read each subtraction word problem, and draw the number of minuends. After that, cross out the subtrahend and count what is left. Also, write the equation below along with the difference.

Mother bought 10 oranges. My sister ate 1 orange. How many are left?

Picture:

Equation:

_____ - _____ = _____

Johnny bought 9 candies at the store. He gave Emma 2 candies. How many candies are left?

Picture:

Equation:

_____ - _____ = _____

Patty bought 7 doughnuts. She gave me 2. How many doughnuts are left with Patty?

Picture:

Equation:

_____ - _____ = _____

MULTIPLICATION

Multiplication is when you take a number and then add them a certain number of times. Here are the parts of a multiplication equation:

MULTIPLICATION NUMBER SENTENCE

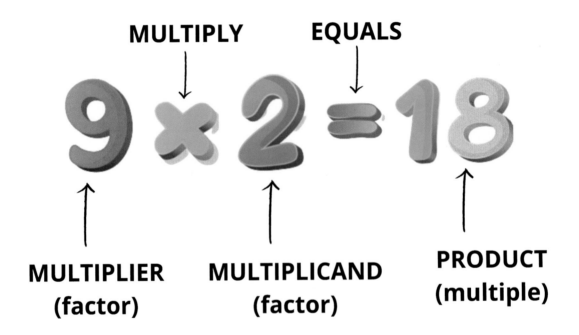

MULTIPLY

EQUALS

MULTIPLIER
(factor)

MULTIPLICAND
(factor)

PRODUCT
(multiple)

The multiplier will be added times the number of the multiplicand to get the product. In this example, you will be Adding the number 9 together for 2 times, which will amount to 18.

Multiplication Equations

Fill in the blanks in the multiplication equation, and refer to the pictures to find the missing parts.

$$5 \times 2 = \underline{\quad}$$

$$2 \times \underline{\quad} = 6$$

$$\underline{\quad} \times 2 = 8$$

$$3 \times 1 = \underline{\quad}$$

$$2 \times \underline{\quad} = 4$$

Multiplication Equations

Fill in the blanks in the multiplication equation, and refer to the pictures to find the missing parts.

$$3 \times \underline{} = 9$$

$$5 \times 1 = \underline{}$$

$$\underline{} \times 2 = 10$$

$$7 \times \underline{} = 7$$

$$1 \times 2 = \underline{}$$

Multiplication Equations

Fill in the blanks in the multiplication equation, and refer to the pictures to find the missing parts.

$3 \times 4 =$ ___

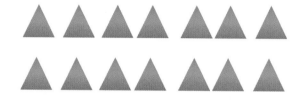

___ $\times 7 = 14$

$5 \times 3 =$ ___

___ $\times 3 = 18$

$6 \times 2 =$ ___

Multiplication Equations

Fill in the blanks in the multiplication equation, and refer to the pictures to find the missing parts.

4 x 4 = ___

___ x 5 = 20

8 x 2 = ___

___ x 9 = 18

10 x 2 = ___

Multiplication Word Problems

Read each multiplication problem. Draw pictures to help you find the answer, and write the multiplication equation along with the product as well.

There are 7 bird cages. Each cage has 1 bird. How many birds are there in total?

Picture:

Equation:

_____ X _____ = _____

My father bought 2 boxes of fruits. Each box has 5 apples. How many apples are there?

Picture:

Equation:

_____ X _____ = _____

A car has 4 wheels. How many wheels will you see if there are 2 cars?

Picture:

Equation:

_____ X _____ = _____

Multiplication Word Problems

Read each multiplication problem. Draw pictures to help you find the answer, and write the multiplication equation along with the product as well.

There are 4 eggs in a tray. What is the total number of eggs if there is only 1 tray?

Picture:

Equation:

_____ X _____ = _____

I have a box with 3 crayons. How many crayons will I have if there are 3 boxes?

Picture:

Equation:

_____ X _____ = _____

A duck has 2 wings. How many wings will there be if I see 3 ducks?

Picture:

Equation:

_____ X _____ = _____

Multiplication Word Problems

Read each multiplication problem. Draw pictures to help you find the answer, and write the multiplication equation along with the product as well.

There are 6 apples in a basket. What is the total number of apples if there are 2 baskets?

Picture:

Equation:

_____ X _____ = _____

My 2 bags are heavy. Each of my bag has 7 books. How many books do I have?

Picture:

Equation:

_____ X _____ = _____

A cat has 1 tail. How many tails are there if there are 10 cats?

Picture:

Equation:

_____ X _____ = _____

Multiplication Word Problems

Read each multiplication problem. Draw pictures to help you find the answer, and write the multiplication equation along with the product as well.

There are 6 candies in a pack. How many candies are there in 3 packs?

Picture:

Equation:

_____ X _____ = _____

A chair has 4 legs. How many legs are there if there are 5 chairs?

Picture:

Equation:

_____ X _____ = _____

There are 7 pancakes in a plate. How many pancakes are there in 2 plates?

Picture:

Equation:

_____ X _____ = _____

DIVISION

Division is breaking numbers into groups of equal parts. These are the parts of the division equation:

DIVISION NUMBER SENTENCE

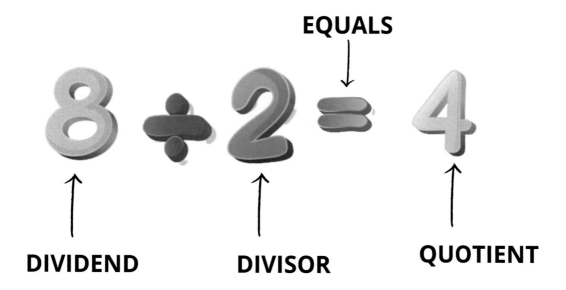

EQUALS

DIVIDEND   DIVISOR   QUOTIENT

You will be breaking down the dividend with the number of groups indicated by the divisor. The number in the groups will be the quotient.

Division Equations

Look at all the items and divide into the groups indicated. Fill in the blanks by writing the quotient of each item.

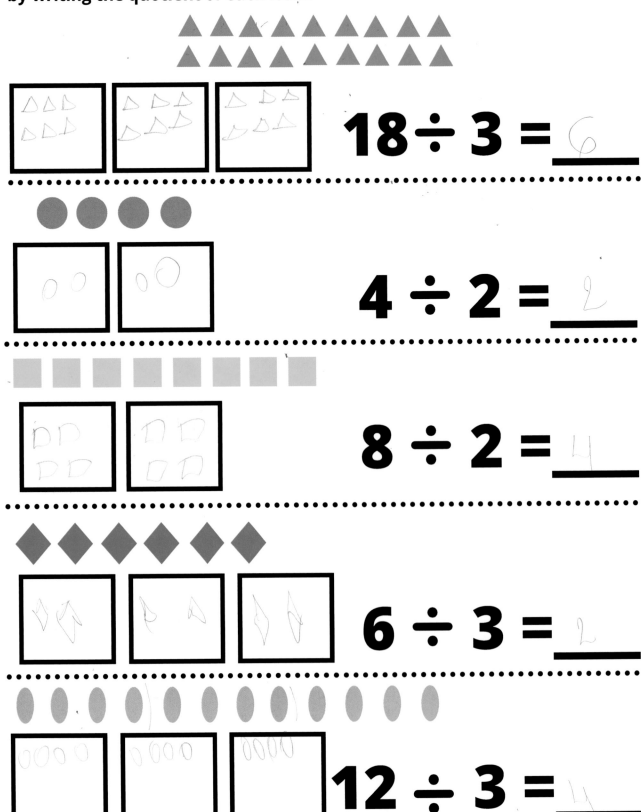

$18 \div 3 =$ 6

$4 \div 2 =$ 2

$8 \div 2 =$ 4

$6 \div 3 =$ 2

$12 \div 3 =$ 4

Division Equations

Look at all the items and divide into the groups indicated. Fill in the blanks by writing the quotient of each item.

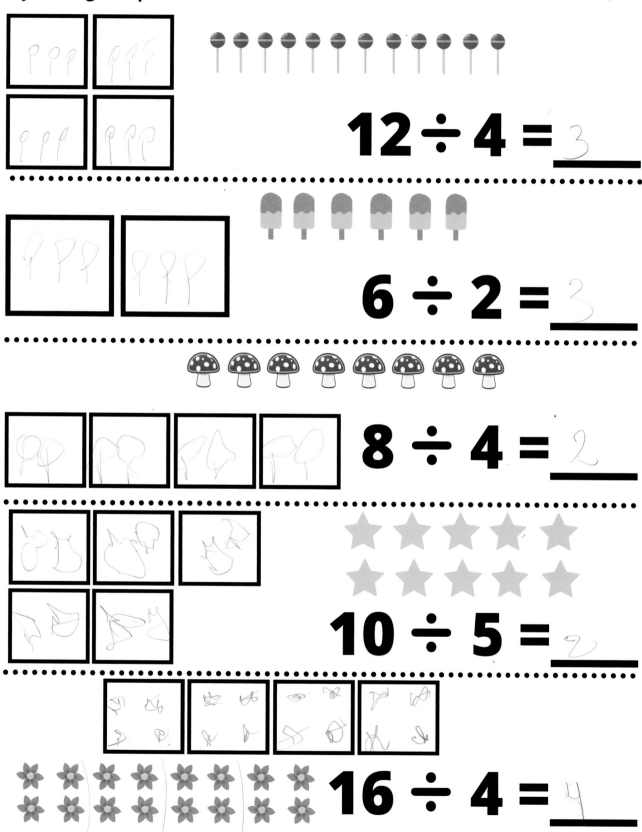

$12 \div 4 = \underline{3}$

$6 \div 2 = \underline{3}$

$8 \div 4 = \underline{2}$

$10 \div 5 = \underline{2}$

$16 \div 4 = \underline{4}$

Division Equations

Look at all the items and divide into the groups indicated. Fill in the blanks by writing the quotient of each item.

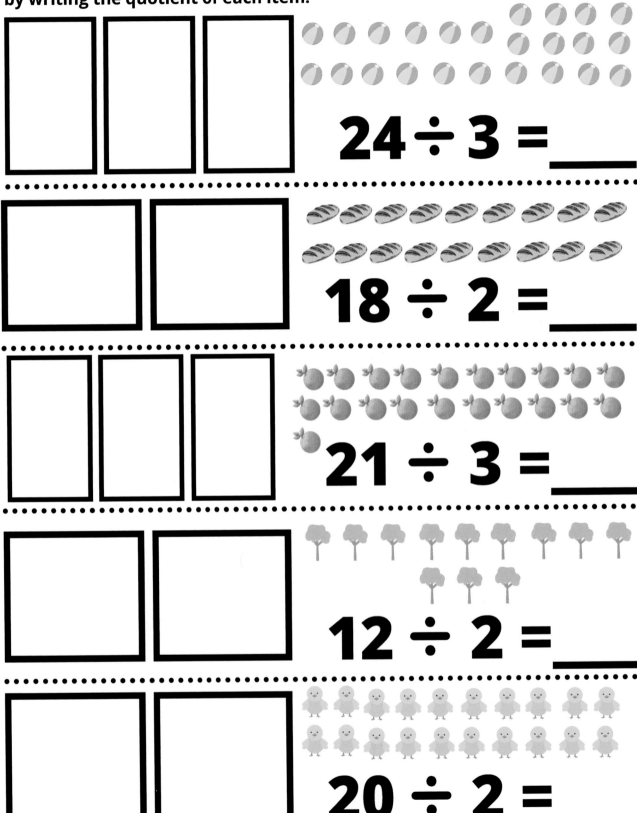

$24 \div 3 =$ ___

$18 \div 2 =$ ___

$21 \div 3 =$ ___

$12 \div 2 =$ ___

$20 \div 2 =$ ___

Division Equations

Look at all the items and divide into the groups indicated. Fill in the blanks by writing the quotient of each item.

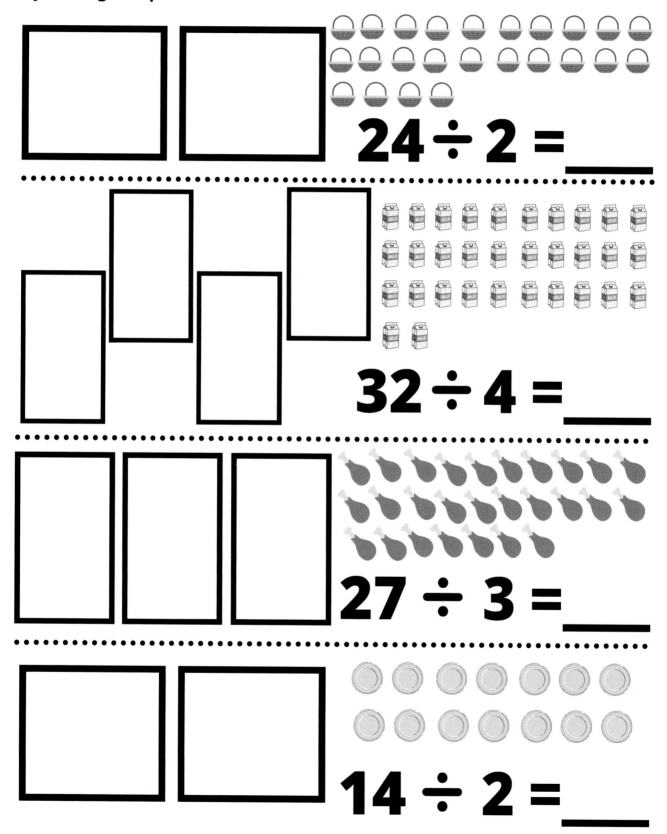

$$24 \div 2 = \underline{}$$

$$32 \div 4 = \underline{}$$

$$27 \div 3 = \underline{}$$

$$14 \div 2 = \underline{}$$

Division Word Problems

Divide the items mentioned into the groups indicated. Draw pictures to help you out. Write the whole equation along with the quotient.

There were 12 apples in a basket. Mary gave the apples equally to her 2 friends. How many apples did each one receive?

Picture:

Equation:

$$\underline{\hspace{4em}} \div \underline{\hspace{4em}} = \underline{\hspace{4em}}$$

A pizza was cut in 8 slices equally shared among 4 people. How many slices did each person have?

Picture:

Equation:

$$\underline{\hspace{4em}} \div \underline{\hspace{4em}} = \underline{\hspace{4em}}$$

Mr. Brown distributed 10 pencils equally among 5 students in his class. How many pencils did each student receive?

Picture:

Equation:

$$\underline{\hspace{4em}} \div \underline{\hspace{4em}} = \underline{\hspace{4em}}$$

Division Word Problems

Divide the items mentioned into the groups indicated. Draw pictures to help you out. Write the whole equation along with the quotient.

Alice baked 16 cupcakes. If the cupcakes were shared equally among 4 of her friends, how many did each friend get?

Picture:

Equation:

_____ ÷ _____ = _____

There are 9 chocolate bars. If I put 3 pieces in a pack, how many packs of chocolate bars will I have?

Picture:

Equation:

_____ ÷ _____ = _____

The baker used 10 eggs to bake 2 cakes. How many eggs were used for each cake?

Picture:

Equation:

_____ ÷ _____ = _____

Division Word Problems

Divide the items mentioned into the groups indicated. Draw pictures to help you out. Write the whole equation along with the quotient.

Simon had 24 pieces of crayons equally packed in 2 boxes. How many crayons were in each box?

Picture:

Equation:

_____ ÷ _____ = _____

Mr. Jones needed to put 30 oranges equally stacked in 3 baskets. How many oranges were in each basket?

Picture:

Equation:

_____ ÷ _____ = _____

There were 16 books equally stored in 2 shelves? How many books were in each shelf?

Picture:

Equation:

_____ ÷ _____ = _____

Division Word Problems

Divide the items mentioned into the groups indicated. Draw pictures to help you out. Write the whole equation along with the quotient.

A farmer owned 27 chickens equally kept in 3 cages? How many chickens did each cage have?

Picture:

Equation:

_____ ÷ _____ = _____

Mother equally packed 21 cookies in 3 bags. How many cookies were in each bag?

Picture:

Equation:

_____ ÷ _____ = _____

The teacher equally divided 22 children in 2 groups. How many children were in each group?

Picture:

Equation:

_____ ÷ _____ = _____

Thank You!

Found this book helpful? Don't forget to give us a 5-Star Review. It helps us create more useful workbooks like these. It also helps our small business thrive. We appreciate it so much!

Made in the USA
Coppell, TX
20 April 2022